To the Dance or the Pools? ~ Virtually!

How different it is to soak at Harbin Hot Springs, than to realize it in virtual Reality

Scott MacLeod
The Making of Virtual Harbin Introduction

To the Dance or the Pools? ~ Virtually!

How different it is to soak at Harbin Hot Springs, than to realize it in virtual Reality

Scott MacLeod

Poetry Press at World University and School
San Francisco and Berkeley

Copyright 2019 by Poetry Press at World University and School
Requests for permission to reproduce material from this work should
be sent to Permissions, Poetry Press at World University and School

Published by Poetry Press at World University and School
PO Box 442, Canyon, California 94516
info@worlduniversityandschool.org
All Rights Reserved

Library of Congress Cataloguing-in-Publication Data
MacLeod III, Scott Gordon Kenneth, 1960-
To the Dance or the Pools? ~ Virtually!: How different it is to soak
at Harbin, than to realize it in virtual reality / Scott MacLeod. p.cm.
Includes bibliographical references and index.
ISBN: 978-0-578-62549-2 1. Poetry. 2. I. Title.

British Library Cataloging-in-Publication Data is available

This book has been composed in Times New Roman

http://worlduniversityandschool.org/AcademicPress.html

Printed in the United States of America

10 9 8 7 6 5 4 3 2

CONTENTS

PREFACE   10

Arriving to Harbin in the mist and rain   13

Illuminated Star Cloud: The dance or the pools? First the dance then the pools   16

Under Stars   20

The coyote is singing to the soft, gray, hazy sunrise   21

Polypore: On the Harbin village path   22

Grapes in Sun: They were cuddling naked on the sleeping deck as I walked into the Harbin pool area today   23

Chaparral: Wind along the road from the town to the springs, and you will come to a gate, talk to them there and enter   26

Pamukkale: Generations of Water   27

Milkweed beetles: Hippy to the Hot Springs & India   29

Lion cuddle: Hippy to the Hot Springs   31

Darwin's Ascension Island: Long welcome spells in the waters 32

Wild *onsen*: Harbin dance 35

Moon sea: Come into the open space Of freedom, of freedom 39

Asclepias milkweeds: Come into the open space of freedom, of freedom, at Harbin, at Harbin 40

Water ~ Into Warmth 41

Gray Langur Troop: Community and Friends 45

The Minarets and Lake Ediza: Harbin Poem Field Notes 46

Dugong and calf: I do choose to write the muse of bliss unfolding 55

The blueness of the sky at night: I do choose to write the muse of bliss unfolding 56

Napa light: It's not just beautiful, it's gloriously sunlit in the north end of the Napa valley 67

Bug on wildflower: Into the warm water hole of Harbin, not the worm hole, New Age, Nyckelharpa 68

Whale flying: Rainy night in Lake County in heading in to Harbin 74

In rainy Napa Oregon Valley I drive through merging worlds 77

Firefly: I came upon a feast of lights spread speckle 'cross hill and vale 78

Wild turkey: Woke up, ... to the Joy of Life 82

Yosemite Valley river: I looked into the valley and saw bliss 85

Pinnacle Rock: The Dirt Road in Lake County 88

Islands and Protected Areas of the Gulf of California: Woke up in Oregon ~ Why do I love thee so? 91

Putorana Plateau, Russia: The sounds go around 95

Blue Grouse: On the road to Harbin ... Naked Anthropologist in Lotus 96

Iberian lynx: Bagpiping to Harbin - A Loving Wedding 100

Ecology happens in front of 7 billion human primates, as philosophers 104

Yellow autumn vineyards blaze below, Green winter oaks above 105

Rolling Lake County Hills: I ride these hills on my way to the waters   109

Amboseli: How different it is to soak at Harbin, than to realize it virtually   115

To the Dance or the Pools? ~ Virtually! How different it is to soak at Harbin Hot Springs, than to realize it in virtual reality   118

Moon setting: Coming home under the moon   126

Day's California brightness and Harbin brilliance resound   127

PREFACE

This little book of poetry, "To the Dance or the Pools? ~ Virtually! How different it is to soak at Harbin Hot Springs, than to realize it in virtual Reality," explores Harbin Hot Springs in a radically new way, - both actually and virtually, and physically and digitally. I wrote many of these poems while I was doing anthropological fieldwork in 2010 & 2011 for my Harbin Hot Springs' ethnographic project, both while at Harbin, and while on the road there, and this book's poems are, in a sense, an expression of this anthropological thinking as well. My large, first book "Naked Harbin Ethnography: Hippies, Warm Pools, Counterculture, Clothing-Optionality & Virtual Harbin" was published in 2016 (in the Academic Press at World University and School), and while it also has some poetry in it, it's an unique ethnographic exploration of both actual and virtual Harbin Hot Springs, coming into conversation with Tom Boellstorff's "Coming of Age in Second Life: An Anthropologist Explores the Virtually Human," (Princeton University Press, 2008). The Academic Press at WUaS seeks also to reinvent the book anew, and to publish eventually from within the Google Street View with time slider environment, text in the sidebar, and planned, with machine translation, to translate all 7,111 known living languages and with virtual Reality (e.g. images and videos) too, to which we can all add, and which will become interactive and with avatar bots. WUaS Press seeks to make this printable to paper too.

The last poem in this book, also entitled "To the Dance or the Pools? ~ Virtually! ... ," is what I'm calling an "idea poem" or "philosophy poem," and possibly as a new kind of genre in poetry, and explicitly explores western philosophy ideas of consciousness.

I hope you, the reader, might be able to 'travel there' or virtually 'visit Harbin' - and via each of the poems in Virtual Reality or VR in something like Google Street View with Time Slider with Maps and Earth and in Google Cardboard, eventually in VR Glasses, thus making it possible to conceive of the book in a new way too, ~ and for any of us to curl up with a good book, and expand our consciousness, in very new ways.

Scott MacLeod
Thanksgiving 2019

Arriving to Harbin in the mist and rain

Arriving to Harbin
in the mist
and rain,

after an amazing
flax seed oil
omega fatty acids'
drive
through the
moist, wet, alive
Napa Valley,
listening to the Dead,

I walk up
past the temple
with the dance,
up through the
wet, dark, verdant garden
and ascend the steps
of Stonefront Lodge.

Walking down past me,
he asks "Are they
dancing down there?"
Nice words :)
Yea, they're dancing,
dancing, dancing
in the temple.

I walk up farther past
the Health Services'
Massage Office and into the
pool area dressing room.
Five women are naked,

here changing,
with no men around right now.
And there's a sculptor I know
who has made
beautiful art
at Harbin.
Oh, and now she in the
dressing room is very pregnant.

Into the waters -
the warm pool
releases so profoundly -
and lovely oneness comes.
I sit in lotus
on the shelf
at the end of the pool
and release,
and release,
into the now~
Home again.

Rain drops
in the pool
form spider webs.
Rain drops
on our heads
bring weather home.
Wet from above,
and the warm
water is all around …

such a fluid world.

Out of the pools,
I walk down to bed.

In the morning,
I awake with money
concerns.

Arising early
on a quiet damp
mid-week morn,
I head into
the empty temple
to explore
the relaxation response.
It's warm and welcoming,
and I sit -
relaxation response
MMmmm. :)

This ocher floor
is a cosmos -
with red galaxies
and brown cloud formations, -
native American earth
in Harbin temple.

http://scott-macleod.blogspot.com/2010/05/red-freesias-arriving-to-harbin-in-mist.html

Illuminated Star Cloud: The dance or the pools? First the dance then the pools

The dance or the pools?

First the dance then the pools.
Long haired folks with
flowing clothes - wild and free.
What a shift -
from the city.

Listen first,
hear the rhythm,
dance a little,
cool, - then away.
Up to the pools,
past the Temple
with its white and
colored lights.

(A woman at the dance
is topless.
She starts to make out with
her friend on the pillows).
How glorious.

And Harbin's evening
illumination is all around.
So soft, - and
so nice to be back ...
Rainbow Gathering? ...
The moon is out,
the garden grasses

are high, and
the air is
fragrant.

I walk up and
there inside
Stonefront lodge,
I see her feet,
for she is lying
on her back
on a sofa, reading.

Past the Gazebo,
under the starlight,
I walk farther
up the way
past Redwood lodge
under the sun deck, and
into the pool area.
Welcome home.
It's dark.

I go into a bathroom,
shut the door,
and write some more -
this here now.

To the warm pool now,
leaving my clothes
on the benches
under the grape arbor.
To the pools.
In,
in ease under,
holding my ears,
float ...
Then to the shelf at one end,
and into lotus pose,
now relaxation response, MMmmm.

Inside, I go deeper -
she's pretty -
then out of the warmth
and into the hot pool.

In the dark,
the candle -
in its holder with holes
that illuminate
a heart image in metal -
looks like a golden brooch
on the neck of the
woman's bust
with flowers in her hair
above the whale spout.

The hot pool is
so beautiful
illuminated by candles
in many ways,
and steam,
in the night,
rises.

And there a woman
sits on
the dolphin railing stairs,
receiving the heat
from this earth's energy.

Out of the pool,
I head to shower,
skipping the
cold plunge,
and walk through
the dark pool area,
cement under foot -

it's joy to be walking
naked here -
to the new little deck
at the far end
of the pool area.
No one is around -
Stars -
then back,
put on my clothes
walk down through
Harbin again,
into the garden,
and past the temple

and to bed.

http://scott-macleod.blogspot.com/2010/05/illuminated-star-cloud-dance-or-pools.html

Under Stars

Under splendid stars,
the smells of oaks
and northern
California tilth,
coming over
the hill from
Napa Valley
to Middletown,
suffuse all air with
earthy fragrance,
welcoming me
back to Harbin land, ~
into the waters soon.

http://scott-macleod.blogspot.com/2010/01/under-stars.html

The coyote is singing to the soft, gray, hazy sunrise

The coyote is singing to the soft, gray, hazy sunrise
over the eastern mountain ranges
- and a cow replies?

Morning sounds, not yet raga

http://scott-macleod.blogspot.com/2010/01/coyote-is-singing-to-soft-gray-hazy.html

Polypore: On the Harbin village path

On the Harbin village path,
I smelled ripe,
wonderful,
green spring.

Oh, the soft moistness,
in the air,
welcomes me
to linger.

Thank you.

https://scott-macleod.blogspot.com/2010/02/polypore-on-harbin-village-path-i.html

Grapes in Sun: They were cuddling naked on the sleeping deck as I walked into the Harbin pool area today

They were cuddling naked
on the sleeping deck
as I walked into
the Harbin pool area today,
along the village path.
Having just awoke,
out of doors,
under the sky,
on comfortable bedding,
they were sharing intimacy
in the morning,
her breast across his chest,
their covers cast aside.
How beautiful.

In the Harbin pools,
50 yards away,
people are often
intimate, naked, cuddling,
but I rarely see this
in other places at Harbin.
The hippie life is good.

The mulberries are ripe and falling.
Try one, they're good, too.

The Harbin pool area -
a musical score for
all of us
bodymind* instruments -
sings.
Look around, feel the sun,

see the naked people,
free on the sundeck,
free under the grape arbor,
find the crescendo,
and let these beautiful
sounds come out, inwardly.
Perch on a bench,
meditate, drink in the
warm pool's fig tree,
the flowers,
the woman wearing a pink sari,
her hair up, - and soar.
She takes it off, and showers,
and goes into the pools.
Play this music in your bodymind.
Synthesize these harmonies,
those accents.
Soak in the waters
for the fermatas.
Do nothing. Be.
Coda.
Come home and resonate.

The music is all around,
for you to practice with,
for you to improvise with,
for you to create your own music.
Play on . . . be creative.
Sing.

The musical scores
are endless here
at Harbin.
How can I appreciate thee more?
What is this neurochemistry?
Upon departing, there,
in the garden,
a guitar and a mandolin player
are jamming.
Jam inside with them.

Ease close,
and sing quietly with them.

The temperature is perfect
at Harbin.
Nature is all around.
There's freedom here, -
join with, and harmonize.
Bring the music home.

http://scott-macleod.blogspot.com/2010/06/grapes-in-sun-they-were-cuddling-naked.html

Chaparral: Wind along the road from the town to the springs, and you will come to a gate, talk to them there and enter

Wind along the road from the town to the springs, and you will come to a gate

Talk to them there and enter

Wander up the way to the pools where we gather, to rest in the beauty of the waters

You and we change, releasing into the waters, naked and free

Come home

Sit in the sun on the deck, talk with friends

The dragon-back ridge line, high up away in the close distance, covered with chaparral, is alive in the light

And you are living anew in Harbin harmony

http://scott-macleod.blogspot.com/2010/07/chaparral-wind-along-road-from-town-to.html

Pamukkale: Generations of Water

Generations of Water

I stand in the shower,
a naked, human primate,
with welcome, warm
water pouring
over my cupped,
open hand, up-reaching fingers,
and full, front body ...
and wonder about
all those generations
before me,
in Africa,
in the rainy season,
water pouring over
thousands of
one-after-another
parents and offspring -
naked, primate
ancestors,
before humans
speciated.

This water is
so warm & refreshing,
so welcome & regenerating.

Was that water cold at times,
in the troop I was part of,
huddling under trees,
waiting, waiting, waiting,
mating and mating,

for the next day, -
not symbolizing,
all the while
through time?

Ötzi,* caught in frozen water,
some 5300 years ago,
in what is now a Swiss glacier,
arrowhead in his left shoulder,
found human, watery coldness,
at life's end.

We humans can talk,
and we can make,
for example,
Harbin Hot Springs'
warm pool,
a basin for receiving
earth-warmed waters,
in which hippies do soak
(and internally sing),
when it's warm or cold.

That beautiful
Harbin canyon,
shady & cool too,
in the heat of summer,
far from the city,
welcomes us human primates now, -
water around
your whole bodymind,
inside & out, -
easing us &
freeing us home.

http://scott-macleod.blogspot.com/2010/10/pamukkale-generations-of-water.html

Milkweed beetles: Hippy to the Hot Springs & India

Hippy to the Hot Springs
meets hippies in the hot springs,
- floats.

Hippy to the Hot Springs
greets hippies in the hot springs
without song. They do Watsu.

Hippy to the Hot Springs
seeks hippies in the hot springs.
She's interested - Love.

Hippy to the Hot Springs
finds hippies in the hot springs, -
cuddle puddle.

Hippy to the Hot Springs
at Harbin Hot Springs, -
plays, easing home.

Hippy to the Hot Springs
finds waters &
generates kindness.

This is a main theme for my Harbin ethnography.

In many ways, folks in India - Hindus and others - are Ur, or first, hippies, in their taking life lightly, in their colorfulness, in their belief in many Gods and Goddesses. Why not? - the more the merrier.

It's culture ...

I come to Harbin and learn.

http://scott-macleod.blogspot.com/2010/10/hippy-to-hot-springs-and.html

Lion cuddle: Hippy to the Hot Springs

Hippy to the Hot Springs

Hippy to the Hot Springs
meets hippies in the hot springs - floats.

Hippy to the Hot Springs
greets hippies in the hot springs
without song - they do Watsu.

Hippy to the Hot Springs
seeks hippies in the hot springs.
She's interested - Love.

Hippy to the Hot Springs
finds hippies in the hot springs -
cuddle puddle.

Hippy to the Hot Springs
at Harbin Hot Springs, -
plays, easing home.

Hippy to the Hot Springs
comes home
in warm waters &
generates kindness.

http://scott-macleod.blogspot.com/2010/10/lion-cuddle-hippy-to-hot-springs.html

Darwin's Ascension Island: Long welcome spells in the waters

Long welcome spells in the waters :)
~ Long Welcome Spells in the Waters

Naked & ur,
Primal, & free from clothes,
Head into Harbin's waters,
Into the welcome, warm pool ~
Now.

{I saw a woodpecker,
black & white,
as I awoke in my car,
skating up the
lower side of a trunk -
light taps reverberating
through the air -
at work,
making a living}.

Everybody is heading
to Burning Man's
freedom in the desert,
and I head to Harbin
which is quieter now,
mid-week, - still summer.

In the cave-like,
temple's rest room,
I stand on an

amazingly beautiful,
stone floor,
while floating on
its deep-wavy, ocean walls,
rose-ocher in color,
looking through
its three round windows -
two of which are portals -
and its one round mirror,
and see Harbin,
beautiful Harbin.
A domed, peaked door,
a copper banister snaking
behind the toilet,
one timber post,
supporting the wood slat ceiling,
irregularly shaped,
I revel in its loveliness.

Up to the pools, soon ...

My anthropological
field site,
Harbon's warm pool,
becomes a water site,
where water work
transforms field work
~ poolside ~
into pool play,
ethnographically.

... took at least
three spells of long,
welcome lingering
in the waters
to release into ease, -

to free into bodymind,
floating, flying,
lotus brain.

http://scott-macleod.blogspot.com/2010/10/darwins-ascenion-island-long-welcome.html

Wild *onsen*: Harbin dance

Harbin Dance

Evening

In the beginning of the dance,
people move easily, slowly & freely.

I see a lot of yoga poses this eve,
and creative asana, too - O, Harbin ...

... and, here, some friends.
People start to stand & sway,

and *amis* move widely,
their beautiful clothes

flowing freely all the while,
dancing, dancing, dancing.

This music moves me not,
so as {hippie} Harbin,

dance freedom
unfolds, all around -

people exploring moving
energy, in their freedom -

I head for the pools,
to soak.

My ear, my right ear,
has had pressure for days,

so, this eve - a first -
I don't submerge,

thinking babying my ear
seems clear-ly sensible.

It's different - head under
for me, is transformative -

I miss going under,
yet my ear is thankful.

To bed, after the hot pool,
and what ideas came in water?

Add the non-theist Friends'
Google Docs' correspondence to

World University & School's
Non-theist Friends' subject?

Generate loving bliss communications,
similar to these,

as correspondence conversations,
as well ? :)

Day

The day is autumn-y,
cool, fresh, but not cold.

How can we all get to loving bliss,
secularly, when and as we want it,

because we are content & well,
and bliss's qualities are elicit-able,

by music, a series of tones, MDMA,
affection from & for another?

Loving friends seem to be the limiting thing,
and sex can help with bliss.

Friends can generate this, but,
furthur, what practices lead

to rocking out?

To submerge in the waters soon,
this poem's monologue may

move to curious, silent communication,
with others, in the warmth, communally,

and voice-free, ~
in the Harbin warm pool,

with its own music.

People's nakedness here
is welcome, freeing & beautiful.

Thank you, Harbin,
for your warm pool's voice,

your countercultural music,
your real freedom

via naked bodyminds, and intimacy,
all around, and warm water's

relaxation response,
via - dare I say ... meditation,

natural & watery? Nay, -
the relaxation response is apropos,

and better, yea, just
soaking in the warm pool.

How to soar, to fly, neurophysiologically ...
and with Harbin as music ~

in new ways?

Don't just read this,
I invite you

- wherever you are -
to elicit loving bliss anew. :)

To the pools - now -
Is this ethnography?
Is this anthropology

of warm water meditation,
of traveling to the *onsen*

for freedom & regeneration?
To the waters, now ...

http://scott-macleod.blogspot.com/2010/10/wild-onsen-harbin-dance.html

Moon sea: Come into the open space Of freedom, of freedom

Come into the open space
Of freedom, of freedom,
At Harbin, at Harbin.

The garden, the garden,
has so many forms there,
of abundance, of shape,
so many species & breeds,
In autumn, in the garden,
in the space which is Harbin.

http://scott-macleod.blogspot.com/2010/10/moon-sea-come-into-open-space-of.html

Asclepias milkweeds: Come into the open space of freedom, of freedom, at Harbin, at Harbin

Come into the open space of freedom

Come into the open space
Of freedom, of freedom,
At Harbin, at Harbin.

The garden, the garden,
Has so many lives there,
Abundances & shapes,
Wild, oft-symmetrical,
Plant-informed forms, -
Space creations, -
A seed spaceship here,
An in-earth,
Water mingler there, -
So many organisms & breeds,
Varieties & hybrids, -
And lovely, native species -
In autumn, in the garden,
At Harbin, at Harbin.

Up to the pools,
At Harbin, in Harbin ...

http://scott-macleod.blogspot.com/2010/11/asclepias-milkweeds-come-into-open.html

Water ~ Into Warmth

Even

Brown leaves are on the ground,
And Harbin is quiet-cold in mid-November,
Yet still the pools draw, and ease,
Us home in waters' beauties ...

Into the warm water ...

Kissing us,
These waters
Ease & cleanse & free, -
And we open in the eve,
Bathing in the warmth,
And, oh, come home ...

In Morning

Receptive rhythms are all around -
Folks coming out from morning yoga, and ...

This temple,
Near which I awake,
Is a rose,

- a cobb & straw bale splendor -

And up there,
In the pool area,
Is watery wonder

- a warm, blue easy-world -

Flowing forth from earth ...

Into the warmth, and out, at ...

Harbin, in which I butterfly awake,
In my car-cocoon,

- MMmmm, the cool, autumn night -

Now, with rising sun,
Is hot, in the morn ...

So many women are beautiful here ...
One walks by, near the temple,
With her clothes on -

We are all naked in the pools,
Where her nudity sings to me -

And, whiling, most genders find
Clothing-optional ease
Here, at home, in Harbin ...

Into the warmth, and out, at Harbin, where ...

Young women ease,
Take off their clothes,
And find freedom, here,
To soak ...

Oh, the countercultural '60s,
From whence this comes,
And by which
New communal forms
Do emerge -

Thanks to social change ...
And we find
Open, nude intimacy,
Here, more free
At Harbin
Than in the
Norms of modernities ...

What, ahead, will change bring? ...

Writing, writing beautiful Harbin,
A place, a valley,
A vision, a song,
A reality ...

Yet loving bliss doesn't yet
Abound for me, or we,
Or us, or here -
Like wondrous, bow strokes
Over Yo-Yo Ma's
Bach-light, cello strings,
Creating sonorities

- yea the music -

Of our neurophysiologies,
Flowing together ...
Fourhands' Guitar, yes,
Any time, with time,
In time, ~ now & together ...

Into the warmth, and out, at Harbin, where ...

Improvisational, countercultural
{raga?} virtuosity, ~
With Bonobo life,
Finds home in
Harbin's warm waters,

On which golden
Fig leaves fall
In the autumn.

http://scott-macleod.blogspot.com/2010/11/water_11.html

Gray Langur Troop: Community and Friends

Community and Friends

Community and friends
seem so disparate, and
Harbin's waters are one.

Where are the collectives,
the houses of students,
the island communities,
of vision and change
for the good,
in web time?

Cold was the night,
and I got in late,
yet the warm pool brought
me home, again.
She who is nude-beautiful,
and we who soak together,
all presence found in
the warmth.

http://scott-macleod.blogspot.com/2010/12/gray-langur-troop-community-and-friends.html

The Minarets and Lake Ediza: Harbin Poem Field Notes

Harbin Poem Field Notes

Rainy December
it is,
but not cold,
and Harbin's
transformations are ahead.

... stop here, stop there,
work on the Web,
on the way.

... stop in Middletown,
for more internet,
before heading in,
up,
on that dark, beautiful
road, at night,
in wintery California.

Oh, the warm pool calls.

Traveling in,
in 2010,
long after the '60s -
yet still here in freedom -
this journey is
soon to become watery.

I like Harbin in winter
because it's quiet, -
but there are
a lot of cars

in the lower, parking lot
this eve.
And I like Harbin
in warmer times,
more than other
Hot Springs around,
like Wilbur & Orr,
because there are a lot
of people here, and
Harbin's culture
is free & funky,
and everybody is out
naked on the sun deck,
in the pool area ...
like our primate ancestors,
in the sun?

Bliss
all the time
eludes -

prepara3ion for
having a family?

- and, moreover, loving bliss
neurophysiology
- both nature & biology -
I invite,
fulsomely,
alone,
and with her,
as duet, -
yet practices
for this
welcome focus,
and this pair-bonding flow
hasn't simply happened,
yet again,
together, with her,

for kids,
especially.

At the Harbin
Gatehouse
(my playful friend is there:)
- no guest pass tonight -
I checked in
{to The King of Hearts' asylum:},
for $25 midweek for 24 hours,
for camping,
for one

(I'm a member of Heart Consciousness Church -
$30 per year, or $10 per month - my goodness,
and here, at Harbin, for comparison,
the most expensive cabin, Cedar,
costs $300, for two,
on a weekend night),

and signed those
Harbin, check-in forms.
Two films, posted there
at the Gatehouse,
are showing this eve:
The Love Play of the Gods,
about sublime, erotic,
1000-ish year old,
Khajuraho in India,
made by an Indian,
and 'Inception,' ...
all for Harbin, film journey-ings
in that hippie theater,
with big pillows, and all,
where it's warm -
but I arrived too late,
and missed the films ...
nice, film titles, though.

Happy to have arrived,
I turn on my hazard lights,
blinking amber in color
- like bus lights in India -
and drive on,
calling out my window,
to my friend at the gate,
'I like the Dr. Seuss
Christmas Tree lights
on top of the Gatehouse.'
Out back, he smiles and waves -
maybe he didn't hear me.

Parking near the temple,
I put down the back seat,
and, oh, find some
whole grain salad
in mustard vinaigrette,
and a hard-boiled egg,
in a cloth, co-op bag,
still good from another time,
inflate my camping pad
in the car,
and pull out my
two sleeping bags, -
I like to be warm
when I sleep.
Ready for bed,
I journey up
through beautiful Harbin
to the pools.

There's a column
of light inside the temple.
I've not seen this before.
What's happening there?

Up I head,
in,
toward the pools,

lingering by the mullein
in the garden, and,
there in the dressing room,
she is ...
naked, with purple towel, -
nipples erect, as I head out
the door into the warm pool,
looking in through the window.
Harbin is wondrous ...
and seems
to open ways for normalcy
of attraction between people,
where the city, and social life,
in modernities,
do not ...
Harbin frees open
the naturalness of sexuality
in a safe place & milieu ...
and women,
yes, women particularly,
welcome this,
and come.
Women open at Harbin -
Goddesses in the
language of
New Age
Harbin.
There are so many
naked women here,
and men, too,
- over the decades, as well -
why is this so rare,
in societies?
Oh, the '60s were about
change, and questioning norms,
and doing things differently, and
about hippies going
to hot springs,
and taking off their clothes.
Peace, love & happiness,

\- a lot of wild explorations
have happened at Harbin, man -
and a big party,
to you.

This cultural connectedness
which is Harbin,
and the transformations
arising from
its milieu,
its pools,
its spirituality,
its service, *satsang* & meditation,
its eclectic-ness,
its freedom from the '60s ...
rocks in its warm pool's
calm, mindful ease,
and naturalness.
Life is good and easy
here at Harbin.

The warm pool was serene,
with 5 people in different places,
all naked, naturally,
under water,
when I went in -
all easing, freeing, being -
on a December night,
in northern California.
No one was cuddling, -
how surprising.
She drifts toward the steps
to the hot pool -
up, out, and in -
Silence, and still, warm waters,
are all around.
Back in the dressing room,
she is bending forward -
her breasts are pendulously-lovely;
another couple dresses and leaves.

Back to my car-cocoon,
for sleep.
The column of light in
the temple -

there was an evening workshop ...

was it an upright, fluorescent bulb,
in a wood casing,
for concentration practices? ...
is one guess,
like Stan Grof's natural,
psychotropic, breath-work
workshops,
which I've participated in
in this temple -

is now off,
and people are putting
away their regenerative,
yoga pillows,
- for finding comfort
on that ocher,
cosmic floor.

Harbin is pretty easy-going,
expectations-wise ...
seems to have drunk of
some do-nothing-ness,
of primate-generations
around watering holes
on African savannahs,
of the wisdom of the 1960s,
and, of warm waters, -
as a now hot springs'
retreat & workshop center.

Ishvara bumped into me last week
in the warm pool,

in the eve.
He's rarely there
at that time.
I was glad - I meditated
right then there in
the waters
(was going to do this anyway :),
while he was doing simple twists,
at pool's end, -
and was also surprised.
Although he lives at Harbin,
I rarely see him.
Harbin is a beautiful, unfolding,
clothing-optional,
hippy vision, which is
also financially successful,
thanks to him, -
and since 1972.
Oh, the warm pool.

And shall we create
all this, too, further,
in a virtual world, ~
a virtual Harbin?

*

These Harbin field notes,
as poetry,
seek lyricism.

*

Tomorrow
as I leave,
I'll get out of the car
at the Gate,

hand in the pass
taped to my windshield,
and drive down the
beautiful, Harbin road,
in the dark.

*

And from the speakers ...

the Greateful Dead are jamming, ~
Fire on the Mountain ~
peaking, improvisation-ally,
at this moment,
And I, transformed
by Harbin,
peak & peak, too,
while listening
to that place's
warm music
in my bodymind,
and the jamming inside.

http://scott-macleod.blogspot.com/2010/12/minarets-and-lake-ediza-harbin-poem.html

Dugong and calf: I do choose to write the muse of bliss unfolding

I do choose to write the muse of bliss unfolding

https://scott-macleod.blogspot.com/2010/12/dugong-and-calf-i-do-choose-to-write.html

The blueness of the sky at night: I do choose to write the muse of bliss unfolding

I do choose to write the muse of bliss unfolding

I do choose to write the muse
of bliss unfolding,
Grateful Dead jamming,
{of raga, too},
a departure from
Pan troglodytes' fighting,
that common chimp-like,
human wont, -
and eat the flax seed
oil oft for omegas,
and revel in their
harmonies & brightnesses,
of this vegetarian lack,
which, with flax,
an egg or two,
regular, good nights' sleep,
and a multi-vitamin
for B12 and iron,
is balanced out,
and accounted for,
with wellness and
via movement.
O, non-harming,
and goodness!

And so I head for
Harbin,
in its freedom ...
and for contact improv,
and dance,

and back country wilderness,
and world travel,
and the extraordinary,
and music-making,
and loving bliss,
and look to generate
friends, in time,
with fulsome,
social interaction
of & with children,
mine and hers, -
to be.
Affection!

Leaving loneliness
behind, - and freedom, too? -
we talk sympathetically, &
I, too, open to the music of
here & now,
and 'flow,' ...
and all this also, ahead,
still singly,
yet more with friends.
The warmth
of loving,
of trusting,
of familiar bodyminds
in proximity,
who use language
with care,
draws me out of
my solitary freedoms,
from people's upsets
and irrationalities,
and tired-nesses,
and my own, -
while seeking
to generate
a freshet of love.

Ah, music, raga,
and the Grateful Dead.

In community,
with friends,
how generate we
both engaged and calm,
raga-like, warm, human,
social interaction?

Writing the muse
of bliss unfolding ...

30 years-playing-together -
having fun -
Grateful Dead improvisations
of their own,
psychedelic music,
with Deadheads who
find ongoing,
communal bliss, -
all together, now.

How grow we
- and practice -
this wonder,
this loving bliss code,
of which the Dead's music
is one example, -
in so many,
new ways?
This seems
noble & worthy, yes, -
and sensible & wondrous, too.
But how, and with whom,
and with which different musics,
both communally & creatively?
Really.

Guidelines for Practicing

Loving Bliss Like
Practicing a Musical Instrument,
to begin?

Traveling on farther now,
through the north end
of the Napa valley,
I play again that
1969 Grateful Dead,
Fillmore music, which
peaks & rises
in, oh, such
hippy-
{almost India-like}
illuminated,
color-filled,
sparkling ways,
emanating forth
from sound speakers.
Coming inwardly &
homeward with music,
I travel on
toward Harbin ...

Intimacy yes,
Bonobos
{Pan paniscus}
not, for me, -
love, yes,
and with words,
awareness & chemistry ...
- a 50 year, Grateful Dead,
fun duet,
I'll cultivate.
Let's innovate,
with pair-bonding ...
two hours a day
of massage &
love-making,
much wondrous coitus,

with each other,
for decades ahead -
far less than Bonobos -
... as bodymind,
musical instruments,
practicing and playing ~
with lots of lingering
in contact, together.
MMmmm ...

The eve is warm,
the night is light, -
it's wintertime
in Napa's valley ...
& up over the hill
I go
to Harbin.
These words
do point
to bliss,
yet, as words,
they don't head
unfolding-ly -
explicatus -
into this ongoing,
exploratory jam,
which the Dead play,
so enjoyably, -
musicians
communicating
together,
responsively & reciprocally -
listening all the while
to one another -
as their generative voices,
and electric instruments,
in tone, weave a beauty,
for we who listen.
What sounds!

I want to write with -
rock and roll poetry -
synthesizing
into togetherness.
I, writing, writing, writing,
by the side of the road,
on the way
to Harbin,
with the Dead
in my head,
travel on.

Shall we make
music of this poem?

In, on, in, on,
finding that inner
togetherness with
this music,
that inner synchronicity, -
with sounds -
he starts to sing:
'ice petal flowers revolving ...
shall we go, you and I,
while we can ...
through the transitive
night fall of
diamonds' -
what a trip -
and, that word,
sung with harmony ...
harmonizes me further.

Tones in a sequence,
created by
these musicians -
bliss-communicating
with each other,
and us -
lead me to bliss.

Tones in a sequence
are an opening way
for you and I
to realize bliss,
when and as you want it.
Ah, serial tones!
Choose the music you love,
{and help the poor,
and disadvantaged,
as well},
and turn it on.
What music would you
substitute for the
Grateful Dead,
in which bliss rises
- for you -
and with which
to jam together?
The Beatles?
The Doors?
J.S. Bach, four-hands?
... Bliss now, and,
grow this glowingly.

Shall I start singing,
to come more in synch,
by myself, -
as by harmonizing with, -
and, at the same time,
move away
from only their words,
to co-create bliss?

'St. Stephen' ...
and I drive on,
on this trip
... MMmmm :)

This poem is

just one example
of learning how
to explore
bliss elicitation,
in words,
with music, here, next ...

Here, now -
I arrive at Harbin,
walk along the village path -
and, voila, everybody is out
in the sun
on the sleeping deck,
in January,
mid-week -
maybe 20 people -
in northern California,
naked ...
A little haven,
and nest,
of human primates,
and freedom,
in modernity,
high on a redwood deck,
- regenerating -
through ongoing travel to,
and journeying in,
this hot springs,
in the California winter.
With symbols, touch and tones,
how to cultivate
a flourishing,
loving bliss ecology
of human primates,
over 10,000 seasons?

My bliss neurophysiology
is so imprecise! ...
Alas!

Yet, with warm pool, and release,
practice offers ways
to attune it ...
Let's learn to bliss
with language's and
musical scores' sophistication,
from a space of learned
ease, skill & excellence.
Ah, the relaxation response ...

So I turn on again
the Grateful Dead,
or find my way
to these kinds of
natural highs,
naturally,
exploring awareness,
and the musical score
of the Harbin pool area ...

- or via Scottish bagpipe playing,
which I do, ...
to produce tones
that generate bliss,
at times, myself -
We can do this ourselves ...
O, for focused, easing,
bliss practices.
Is the 'loving,'
in loving bliss,
neurophysiology elicitation,
the limitation?
The ease of
soaking in the warm pool,
of listening to the Dead,
of practicing bliss,
is unfolding-ly
written here now.

When 'flow' comes,

and then more ...
Lift off
... as if in this sunlit world
of warm water release,
with couples cuddling all around -
naked, free, with a friend,
and, in ease, together -
we might play bliss,
and - especially - love.

My evolutionary biological,
Non-theistically friendly,
bodymind neurophysiology
is so imprecise.
A-las!

And still I find
this connectedness
at Harbin
all so easy.

A friend to jam with,
who generates bliss for me,
to which I respond, in kind,
I welcome.

So, yes ...
how, further, to get to the
neurophysiology of loving bliss ...
like Ma's cello bow strokes,
playing sweet Bach?
... or 30 years of
Grateful Dead jamming -
a bunch of guys
improvising, playing,
and having fun
with one another,
which Deadheads love -
and making money.
Life is good.

It wasn't always bliss
for them, the Dead,
- they were sometimes 'off' -
or for me,
in this conceiving,
not always ...
- relaxation response,
regularly, ... yes, for
in-tuning our biologies -
but what a lot of
we-create-music-together
bliss ...
and when the Dead
are dialed in,
Jerry and Brent, yes ~
Going Down the Road Feeling Bad ~
they'd rock,
naturally,
happily,
communally, and
creatively,
all of which we, *oui*,
can grow.

How, now, does the
MDMA-like, cello bow stroke
of loving bliss,
neurophysiology elicitation
work? ...

for I do choose to write the muse
of bliss unfolding.

http://scott-macleod.blogspot.com/2011/01/blueness-of-sky-at-night-i-do-choose-to.html

Napa light: It's not just beautiful, it's gloriously sunlit in the north end of the Napa valley

It's not just beautiful,
it's gloriously sunlit
in the north end
of the Napa valley ...

every glance of light
on a vine,
a musical, moving note :)

http://scott-macleod.blogspot.com/2011/02/napa-alight-its-not-just-beautiful-its.html

Bug on wildflower: Into the warm water hole of Harbin, not the worm hole, New Age, Nyckelharpa

Into the warm water hole of Harbin, not the worm hole

(Field notes)

Into the warm water hole of Harbin,
not the worm hole,
of mind-altering, quantum physics, -
which has its own life at Harbin;
how is this an aspect of culture?

(What are implications
of quantum mechanics'
for neuroscience,
and the brain & bodymind, if any?
Explore this via MIT Open Course Ware at
World University and School's
Neurobiology -
http://worlduniversity.wikia.com/wiki/Neurobiology
- subject page? There aren't any MIT OCW courses that touch on this, yet).

Earlier, I went into the
coffee house in town
for the internet,
before coming up to Harbin,
and my friend was there.
We went to a Chinese restaurant

after web surfing,
and talked
while he had dinner;
I was full.
(The Chinese have contributed
so much to California
in the past 150 years
and don't get the recognition
they deserve.
How to rewrite history?
A golden place of vision,
beauty & opportunity,
California has its racist history, too).

New Age dualisms about
this life and an after life - all one -
abound at Harbin.
They're part of its church, in a way,
and in 21 dimensions, at times.
While not my
evolutionary biological
non-theistically friendly
(loving bliss-centric)
bodymind neurophysiology
thinking in modernity -
I am nevertheless familiar with New Age
hippy-oneness thinking,
which finds a home at Harbin
in Lake County, California,
in 2010.

I soaked, finding ease,
among naked, fellow travelers,
just passing through Harbin,
flowing themselves through the warm pool,
and walked down through *Mainside**
toward bed.
There in the restaurant

I heard sounds of music.
I went in for water.
Two musicians were playing
the similar instruments,
which I hadn't seen before.
I mentioned to a friend
who was filling up her
hot water bottle there that
the music sounded like
minuet dance music from western Europe.
She asked me what the instrument was.
I said it looks like a very weird
viola da gamba,
or a weird, straight dulcimer,
with piano-like keys on the fret board,
and which is played with a bow.

After listening further -
it was around 10 pm
and only 4 of us were there -
my friend asked the musicians
what the instrument is.
The man said it was
Swedish folk instrument,
a *nyckelharpa**
(a keyed fiddle, I later found out), -
he mentioned that
the Swedish group
'Väsen'
- here's "Väsen Street" -
(https://youtu.be/tWorsJwzycw)
played one,
very nicely, -
and that I could find
their music on YouTube.

An ethnomusicology
of Harbin grows
with this :)

Into the warm water hole
now in the morning.

It's people's energy at Harbin I find so interesting.
Harbin's milieu is somehow very attuned to this,
as am I ... it's kind of a hippy vibe thing -
all coming together as in ongoing, hippy, Harbin oneness.

*

Talked with a friend this morning
who was interested in
Brainfingers.com in reverse.
Brainfingers* allows you to communicate
with a computer screen interface
to pick letters from a screen keyboard,
or play games,
WITHOUT language or hand movements,
but instead by something like 'brain signals.'
I've tried it once in Greece, and it worked,
and it seems legitimate, although rudimentary.
And the inventor has brought it to
Stephen Hawking who has Lou Gehrig's disease, to try it,
and who was too agitated to use it successfully.

My friend would like, for example, any
text to go directly into his brain without reading, or listening -
so, Brainfingers in reverse.
As I understand Brainfingers in a simple way from an explanation in 2007,
it involves three biological aspects of the bodymind, which its three sensors work with -
electromagnetic activity, minute eye movement, and something
which researchers don't understand, which the inventor (Andrew Junker), called 'brainwaves.'

So, to understand these three processes in reverse would offer a way to begin to think about how to translate symbols from a page directly into the brain.

Researchers at Dragon Naturally Speaking Voice Recognition, thinking about how this process works IN REVERSE, may have explored aspects of these questions, as well.

http://scott-macleod.blogspot.com/2011/02/bug-on-wildflower-into-warm-water-hole.html

Napa light: It's not just beautiful, it's gloriously sunlit in the north end of the Napa valley

It's not just beautiful,
it's gloriously sunlit
in the north end
of the Napa valley ...

every glance of light
on a vine,
a musical, moving note :)

http://scott-macleod.blogspot.com/2011/02/napa-alight-its-not-just-beautiful-its.html

Whale flying: Rainy night in Lake County in heading in to Harbin

Rainy night in Lake County
in heading in to Harbin ...
Blue moonlight on wet road
illuminating the behind
through the rear view mirror.
I stop for beauty.
Mozart sounds ... what
musical conceptions!
and from long ago,
yet here so now, -
away we go
all over that space
of virtuosity,
I slow in, in wonder,
to Harbin,
soon to soak.
Traveling here,
another poem is coming,
expression finding
flower form
like water traveling
up from ground,
seeking pool to warm
and seep into
all those
inner, bodymind recesses,
that welcome ease
and flourish in.

There's freedom & agency
in writing poems -
to write what one likes,
to sing the song
one wants to,

to fly in the warmth
of word music,
intimate, lyrical & free -
and inhabit those
rosy spheres,
or what you will,
which differs from
the freedoms
of being a Doctor,
a M.D.,
or an Anthropologist,
with their languages.
Exploring other
languages & spheres
is possible
with these knowledges,
but these freedoms
aren't inherent in
knowledges' discourses.
Poetry writing offers
an autonomy -
but by which especially! ...
when you find
your voice
of poetry ...

Snow in the morning -
beautiful snow
on the evergreens
above the creek
over the bridge
to the Conference Center,
out the door of my car,
where I awake,
in quiet, wintery Harbin ...
bodymind music with Harbin.
I see in this falling snow
among the conifers, -
in nature, -
a beautiful philosophy of

Gia-fu Feng's 'Tao te Ching,'
which flourishes
with Jane English's photos ...

Up to the pools
'cause it's cold out,
and the day is alive.

http://scott-macleod.blogspot.com/2011/02/whale-flying-rainy-night-in-lake-county.html

In rainy Napa Oregon Valley I drive through merging worlds

In rainy Napa Oregon Valley
I drive through merging worlds,
of wet and green and beautiful
fresh gray natural
toward the even more
watery world of Harbin's
non-commune, communal pools.
(Bring this home yourself :)

Smiling while traveling
hair is soft
yet smiles
aren't
frequent enough.

What will emerge
this time
in Harbin world?

http://scott-macleod.blogspot.com/2011/02/in-rainy-napa-oregon-valley-i-drive.html

Firefly: I came upon a feast of lights spread speckle 'cross hill and vale

I came upon a feast of lights spread speckle 'cross hill and vale

I came upon a feast of lights
spread speckle 'cross hill and vale,
and reveled
in their evening softnesses.
And from Harbin's redwood,
sleeping deck, below,
I saw Gazebo's
octagonal lights,
on *Mainside*, -
a tasty, illuminated pie, -
ready to spin-off
in a wee-wee :)
psychedelic-whirligig,
through starry cosmos,
but, instead,
centers this
Harbin-light,
beauty gaze,
in winter,
at night,
from here.

I walked in on that dark,
empty, village path, at night.
No one was around ...
It would have been easy
to stumble upon
some jutting rock,
but I didn't,

and so came to this
way-place
of glimmering,
night-light beauty, -
this redwood deck,
which, so full in the day
with resting,
naked bodyminds,
in solace-ease
from stresses of modernities,
gives forth these
welcoming visions
of la lumière.

Heading now
into the pool area,
I bring this light
show with, and in,
my bodymind,
to venture deeper
into mysteries
of aliveness, -
naked, warm and free -
in Harbin's watery warmth.

Where are you now,
my love,
with whom this all to share,
and rock out in with,
all together?

And, oh, what beautiful orchards
of ripe, fruit, human living! ...

Pools now,
in warm-oneness-ease ...

Heading on in now ....

What delight this night,

in this very warm pool!
Why this particular,
bodymind joy,
this eve?
Nothing special ... don't know ...
Was it because I talked,
and connected,
with a smart, receptive friend,
in words, about loving bliss,
on the phone coming up?
We thought out loud about
this bliss-love:
Ecstasy is MDMA,
methylene dioxy meth amphetamine, -
theoretically,
a love-everything-in-the-world-intensely,
for 5-8 hours,
biochemical, bodymind,
reference experience
for 75% of we ingesters, -
for affective euphoria, -
and one,
of so, so many,
replicable qualities of bliss,
for we who are biological beings, -
symbolizing, human primates,
shaped by evolution
by natural selection.

And we talked further about
Scottish Country Dancing,
which we've done together,
quite long ago,
with bliss,
via its ebullient
series of tones,
its music, movement,
and sociable interactive-ness.
It's a related, also replicable -
like technology, - example.

Was it, too, the Ginseng tea,
earlier today, of which
I hadn't drunk in a while?

Still, the weather of my bodymind
hasn't yet found its
cello bow strokes
of loving bliss agency,
of this music-making,
here and now,
when desired.

And as I write,
and while in concert hall,
of this Harbin warm pool, -
my bodymind, yes,
is conducive to such bliss,
yet, I haven't caused
these joys.

What can cause bodymind,
loving bliss, whenever, but,
especially, here now?

I do, though,
like this weather,
here tonight,
in winter,
at Harbin.

http://scott-macleod.blogspot.com/2011/03/firefly-i-came-upon-feast-of-lights.html

Wild turkey: Woke up, ... to the Joy of Life

Woke up, ... to the Joy of Life

Woke up
to a single, male turkey
in full, feather display,
gliding across the top
of a little, grassy ridge,
with a rounded,
colorful bodymind,
in dominant, alpha moment,
above, in the distance,
with California oaks
all around,
- it's an old scene.

(Why here now? ...
I don't know turkey biology ...
Was it because I opened
my car door,
that it strutted its stuff?
Is it mating season?
... didn't see any turkey hens nearby,
although they probably weren't far).
At the end of its glide,
it transformed itself
back into its
halt-walking,
vulture-like,
strange-torpedo,
missile-body
self-shape,
and clucked a little.

Waking by the side
of the road,
in rural California,
after a star-illuminated,
gorgeous night,
outside Harbin
where I sometimes camp, -
is this single, male Turkey
in full display,
a spiritual awakening?

And how is it possible to
observe this California,
natural-world moment,
as musical notation,
for bodymind bliss-elicitation?
Starry night walk, yes, - a little?
Turkey-glide-display, - not so much?

(There's something about
wild turkeys' appearances
I find unappealing).

So, were I to have gotten close,
but not too close,
to observe its beautiful feathers,
with near perfect round-symmetry,
in all brown, black, beige, white and rust colors,
with its blue face, and red, bulbous throat for warbling,
little shimmery, green feathers throughout,
with 5 inch long, pendant, chest feather,
its head, in the middle,
a little above center
of its tail display,
I might have merged
my mind into this natural,
for-observing Turkey Mandala of
male, spiritual now-ness -
with appreciation, -

to come again later.

But this isn't the bliss,
for example,
I know from Mozart, the Grateful Dead,
or Matisse's 'Joy of Life'
or in flower photography's beauty,
or, especially, in the easing release
of the Harbin warm pool,
into one kind of contentment,
with naked people
coming into and out of it,
all around.

I open the car door again,
and this male turkey is gone.

MMmmm, ... natural, loving bliss
draws me fulsomely,
and this natural world
is opportunity to explore
bliss anew.

Wake up your biology of bliss,
Wake up your loving neurophysiology.
Music, nature and nudity, especially,
are all notational scores, -
improved upon with
loving, smart conversation,
and, even better, with singing,
with friends -
for heading into the
easing waters of musical joy.

http://scott-macleod.blogspot.com/2011/03/woke-up.html

Yosemite Valley river: I looked into the valley and saw bliss

I looked into the valley and saw bliss

I looked into the valley
and saw bliss,
in Napa,
upon leaving Harbin, for a spell.

It's the light on the dormant vineyards,
the wild hills just behind,
the Dead on the sound system,
the Omega 3s from flax,
and the driving ...
O, Napa and Harbin.

Things are mellow,
there's jamming in the air,
and I was wondering,
just a little bit ago,
while in the pool, warm,
whether the Harbin pool area itself
is a human, visual, Bonobos
forest-in-the-pool thing, -
erotically, yes.
Are we all left-bank, Sapiens primates,
rocking out, Bonobo-wise,
on Harbin's clothing-optional-ness, -
such space-releasing wonders, -
the women, especially?
Have we learned,
just a little,
to return
to the freedom
of natural attraction,

while softening in the warm, clean,
bubbling-out-of-ground
waters at Harbin?

The sky is mottled,
with grays, whites and blues,
making vivid yellow grasses
underneath stumps of
lovely grape-potentiality,
in this California winter.

The sun is setting,
on the other side,
of where I be, and
'Dark Star' is playing.
Turn it on,
and jam with
all the way home
from the pools,
to Canyon,
where bed awakes, -
but without her,
so far.

On we so go, -
why this constellation of beauty
in north Napa Valley,
upon leaving Harbin?
Think I'll sing this love,
anew, inventively ...

And the Dead play
on and on ...
what space ~~~~~~~~~ for such long times ...
grooving,
my o my, ...
feels like long orgasm,
but in tones
sustainable,
jubilant,

yet laid back,
and flowing.
They're happening,
and I just sit and wonder
at these ear flowers,
and smile, and write, -
all with, ... while

'Mirror shatters
in formless reflections of matter,
glass dissolving ...

and I, merging and crescendo-ing,
all the way home,
bubble love ~

On & on home ...

http://scott-macleod.blogspot.com/2011/04/yosemite-valley-river-i-looked-into.html

Pinnacle Rock: The Dirt Road in Lake County

The Dirt Road in Lake County

On the dirt road in Lake County, California,
I saw a little, playful head-butting
between two, baby cows, calves,
- were they male or female?
I don't know -
on a beautiful, oak ridge,
near Harbin,
this morn. The oak trees,
dotting the ridge, above them,
in full, spring leaf,
filled out this 'Ferdinand the Bull' scene.
This could easily be Greece, or Spain,
in Mediterranean, inland California,
virtually.
And this baby playfulness,
perhaps 10 cows and calves
all around,
on a perfect day,
has probably gone on
long before that thriving
culture on Samos, Greece,
with its aqueduct,
the 2,540 years old
Tunnel of *Eupalinos*,
- Herodotus's 8th world wonder,
I think -
and long before the first cities
of 10,000 years ago, -
as part of agriculture,
in time immemorial.

Two woodpeckers then alit
on a branch, very close,
black & white, with red heads -
a pair they were, -
then flipped under the branch,
still attached, upside down,
echo-pecked a little,
and flew away, displaying
their magnificent, small, wing spans from
below, black & white,
all spread out, in beautiful expansiveness.

These rolling hills & trees,
a bucolic, pastoral, calming scene,
Ferdinand-peaceful,
after good, needed sleep! ~
such beauty in solo-ness.

The cows are gone, now.

A brown truck,
a little fumy,
with two men of
Spanish-Mexican descent,
drives by on this
wide, beautiful, well-maintained,
dirt road ... They look like
salts of the earth,
one man smiling,
as I too smile at him,
in passing.
Who are they,
in this other world?
Might they have staged
this gentle calve-romp, -
for, soon after the head-butting,
another calf rolled over,
almost playfully,

too cute,
and stood back up,
up on the ridge,
where I had seen turkeys,
of an earlier poem -
through knowledge of, and
skill with, livestock and cattle?

A kid on a too-small, motor scooter,
- that looks like fun,
and this could be Greece, again -
then passes, legs asunder,
hair flying, under his knit hat.
He looks as if he may be
heading to school.
Are his hands cold?

Ranch land, with pasture and oaks,
on both sides of this road,
sun shining, no houses ...
in this out of the way place, -
and Ferdinand is very happy now.

Soon to Harbin ...

Harbin ...
yes ...
It's always different,
its own thing, and
so enlivening.

http://scott-macleod.blogspot.com/2011/05/pinnacle-rock-dirt-road-in-lake-county.html

Islands and Protected Areas of the Gulf of California: Woke up in Oregon ~ Why do I love thee so?

Woke up in Oregon ~ Why do I love thee so?

Woke up in Oregon,
with wild flowers all around,
fragrant, an old orchard, too,
and with beautiful, varied trees,
coming from California,
on my way to the Rainbow Gathering
near the town of Cougar,
in southwest Washington state,
in the Gifford Pinchot National Forest.

Woke up in Oregon ~ Why do I love thee so?

No rain this morning,
in Calapooya,
but the weather is Oregon -
gray and overcast -
in these southern hills,
where I've camped for the night,
by the side of the road.
Why do I love thee so, Oregon?

Two hummingbirds fly close,
and hover ...
no sugar sweetness here, now -
on they navigate in search of food.

The ethos in Oregon of
softness and caring -
with commerce, and in the laws, too -
comes through time,
from my Reed days.
Why, and how, does California contrast?
Where are the remarkable
histories of Oregon's goodness,
and how to grow California's freedoms, abounding-ly?

In Ashland, the food co-op,
in principle,
has grown, and is thriving,
from my People's Food Co-op days,
in Portland, in the first half of the 1980s.
Bicyclists and long-haired men
abound, and curious bubble vehicles, as well.
Unique goods, produced alternatively, fill the shelves.
This food is wholesome & good.
It's nice to linger here,
and I found free internet access
in this co-op, -
with such tasty & healthy food.
Oh, this sourdough French bread was so soft & fresh -
ate a whole loaf down in one sitting.
It's summertime in Ashland,
the weather is good
and the people are out
free on the street,
happy & relaxed
in this small, Oregon city.

Birds arc and swoop low
above the grasses,
and among the Queen Anne's lace,
in the meadow
beyond the gate.

Such skillful, graceful fliers -
playing with time & space,
in flight.

Feeling a little disconnected
and looking for connecting,
I head to Rainbow,
where I learn, as well,
- nearly 40 years after it started in 1972.
Ah, the children of the light,
where people greet each other,
with 'We love you' -
and where there's the cultural freedom
to mean this here now.
It's a festival of hippy
communitas in 2011,
in a forest
in a part of the world
where Rainbow began,
where two tribes, one from the Pacific NW
and one from northern California,
and everybody else under the sun,
came together near Boulder, Colorado,
all these years ago,
as I've heard it told.
I haven't seen any Rainbow vehicles
on the road traveling north so far,
no hippy vans, no colorful freedoms,
no signs of a Rainbow on the road.
A little nervous about going -
hippies can be 'out there' -
what will emerge this year at Rainbow?

Such sweet, moist, fragrant air, ~
are those blackberry blossoms
around that old, beautiful gnarled stump nearby?
The oaks nearby on the golden hill spread,
not psychedelically, but do create such

canopies of comfort and beauty,
their branches spiraling into
into sky.

The dry, bull rush head is close.
No Doug Fir Old Growth forests here,
for this is more Oregon hobbit land,
of beautiful farms and lovely lands.

http://scott-macleod.blogspot.com/2011/07/islands-and-protected-areas-of-gulf-of.html

Putorana Plateau, Russia: The sounds go around

The sounds go around

The sounds go around
in the eve
here in Lake County -
back road country -
as they always have,
for millions of years.

I listen and write,
as the crickets, and related,
creak their age-old songs

...

with awareness, and appreciation
that no humans were here
on Turtle Island,
north America,
more than 20,000 years ago,
to hear this, -

and that early writing
began possibly
only 5,000 years ago.

http://scott-macleod.blogspot.com/2011/07/putorana-plateau-russia-sounds-go.html

Blue Grouse: On the road to Harbin ... Naked Anthropologist in Lotus

On the road to Harbin ...

Naked Anthropologist in Lotus

To Heartsong on his birthday

On the road to Harbin
I lost cell phone contact
with my friend,
in Napa, in autumn,
on a gloriously sunny day.

She told me of a
Nigerian Marimba singer,
with great voice,
who may join their band,
and, very happily, too, of a book
"The Ecstasies of a Lunatic Farmer,"
which might be a nice gift
for Yogini Angelini Angela Farmer.

Right out of the '60s, it seems ...
right on ...

Bubbling over, she herself,
my friend up north,

is flowing ecstasy in
the rhythms of the land,
of her little, paradise farm-let,
while connecting with raising livestock,
and the wholeness of it all.
Cosmos.

The signal dropped again and again,
as I tried to say something about
U.S. universal health care
on the phone,
and World University & School,
along that curvy road.

The day was so illuminated in Napa,
with the vineyards
browning on the ground,
... Beaujolais must abound around
(but I basically don't drink).

Came to Harbin,
with new folks at the Gate,
drove far in, parked,
set up my car camp,
and wandered along that
somewhat random, Village Path, -

for Harbin's village
isn't really a village,
but could be,
(it's just a little row of houses) -

where I met, at start,
a very beautiful woman,
near the bridge,
coming the other way,
dressed only in a green towel,
with beautiful, bare legs,
a harbinger of the pool area

at path's end, to come.

Under the grape arbor,
Off with my clothes, and
Into the warm pool first,
warmth simply
welcoming you in,
again & again, ...

Anthropologist as naked meditator,
sitting cross-legged in full lotus,
which roots you perfectly down,
in those waters,
onto pool bottom,
head just above the water's surface,
like a flower,
in the Harbin warm pool ...
'tis a new way of
thinking of,
of imagining 'the anthropologist'
... Still ...
relaxation response,
connecting with the vibe
of the waters,
the vibe of the warm pool,
of the naked soakers,
some cuddling,
of the beauty of nudity
with participant observation,

and then writing ...
poetry
... anthropologically?

Field work as pool play ... yes.

Watsu ~~~

Connecting in the warm pool,
no dropped signals here,
warm watery welcome home,
in this place of beauty,
of harmonizing oneness,
of attraction, intimacy & nudity ...
of unfolding vision,
of peace in water.

http://scott-macleod.blogspot.com/2011/09/blue-grouse-on-road-to-harbin-naked.html

Iberian lynx: Bagpiping to Harbin - A Loving Wedding

Bagpiping to Harbin - A Loving Wedding

I played a wedding gig
in SF's East Bay, -

where music happened -

and drove off,
right after,
to Harbin,
to play at another
singing, *kirtan* wedding,
turning left on
the Silverado trail, and
into Napa Valley.

Just then,
two motor-cyclers passed me,
and one popped
a big, ride-it-high wheelie, -
hot-dogging free.

Soon after
I called my cosmic friend
up north,
who didn't answer,
so I left a message,
about this previous poem ~
http://scott-macleod.blogspot.com/2011/09/blue-grouse-on-road-to-harbin-naked.html ~
and then came upon
a profusion of cosmos blooms

flowering by the side of the road.
O' purple synchronicity.

Car broke down
a little farther on, -

'check engine light,'
no coolant, -

so got a ride, -
car, me and all, -
to Calistoga,
for some cooling fluid,
and drove on.
(Where is that solar car ...
to reverse global warming?)

Came to Harbin,
checked in as
a wedding guest,
and heard a Marimba band
playing in the Temple, -
polyrhythmic enjoyment,
from Santa Cruz,
which I've blogged about
here before.

Fall is in the air, and
this evening is
first-time
cool, in a while.
O the light
at Harbin is beautiful.

What is this place
called Harbin?
It looks, to me, like a
hippie commune,
building-wise,

but it's not, and
neither is it a country club,
nor a university campus,
(but it could be either),
although there is
a little Watsu school here,
and there's talk of a
New Age University
(both in the recent, last,
Summer 2011, Harbin Quarterly, and
in the 1996 "Living the Future" pamphlet), -
and very alternative, indeed.
A hotel, yes it is, in part, and
a New Age center, and home,
for many, - yes.
An ashram, and two churches,
Heart Consciousness Church,
and New Age Church of Being,
yes, - it is all three,
the latter two, legally.
And - nature - it's a valley with
geo-thermally heated waters
flowing freely from the ground, -
absolutely -
and this makes Harbin
nude beautiful,
and helps turn it into hippie *communitas* ...
Hmmm ... yes.

And yes, most simply,
it's a hot springs'
retreat center,
with many,
long-time residents,
who make up this community, -
where, with a lot of visitors, too,
all here together be.

The natural light on my car,
in the night, is multifaceted,

what a trip, -
as is the light on the ground,
near the driver's door,
and so is the light on the roof.
What illumination!

And Angela may be here,
at the close of her
women's yoga retreat, -
nay, in the middle of it ...
I see some familiar faces,
from previous courses.

The pools soothe,
yet I have a cough,
so don't linger
in them long.

To bed, to rise tomorrow
to play bagpipe for a wedding
of Harbin friends I love.

The wedding is merry,
with warmth and radiance,
where the groom invited us all to sing,
again and again,
and then sang himself -
rock and roll love,
he sang it forth -
while she beamed, ...
both so happy at
connecting in this way,
among we hippy friends.

http://scott-macleod.blogspot.com/2011/10/iberian-lynx-bagpiping-to-harbin-loving.html

Ecology happens in front of 7 billion human primates, as philosophers

Ecology happens in front of
7 billion human primates,
as philosophers ...
Life,
human drama,
water,
the natural world,
symbols,
what you think,
friends
and the extraordinary,
all flow by ...
watch & enjoy & be with ...
explore the relaxation response ...
a lot moves in us

https://scott-macleod.blogspot.com/2011/11/ecology-happens-in-front-of-7-billion.html

Yellow autumn vineyards blaze below, Green winter oaks above

green winter oaks grace hillsides in Napa,
and yellow autumn vineyards blaze below,
on the road to Harbin.

it's late autumn, warm,
and sun is winking through clouds.

orange flares from that orchard,
red sea tops those vineyards, -
this world splashes with color here,
and there, and all around, -
they are startling.

over the hill I come into Lake County,
where more muted are the colors,
woodsy, fall and natural,
a little winter-season grey overhead.

Harbin, next, arrives ... I head far in ...
to the village path, -
it's like hiking again, on it,
and this way is often a little trippy -
I like, but 'tis curious ...
why this subtle psycho-tropism?

at the redwood sleeping deck,
there's lovely, free-person D-A
walking up toward
Tea House,
high on the hill.

We smile,
"I'm going hiking, " she says.

then to the pools,
full, again, in off season, mid-week,
yet Taoist-ily & toast-ily self-regulating ...

soaking, soaking, soaking,
deeply
among the people, -
smiling, ... little bliss qualities emerge ...

out of the pools,
into the shower,
walking down beyond
the swimming pool,
then back to sauna,
where it's warm.

who is that lovely woman,
with healthy feet, in the sauna,
with just a bikini bottom on?
She is slight, mid-length brown hair, ...
beautiful breasts,
yes ...

then out, dressed, and back along the path,
stopping on the redwood, sleeping deck
now at even-time,
with the lights, here, again,
of Harbin, which are so
spread-speckle beautiful, -
soft, warm, light illuminations,
everywhere,
curious fireflies, of sizes' diverse,
and on, steadily,

not flickering, ~
singing their soft and welcome *oms*.

lights at night, Harbin,
a dream of beauty in the woods,
in this valley,
around pools of warm water,
in which people soak, naked and free,
cuddling their energies together,
in quiet joy, with intimacy.

I head on ...

walking back to my far-in vehicle,
move it to a more central, parking place,
across from the middle parking lot, ...

to play music,
on my bagpipe practice chanter,
on my car's tailgate, -
eve is still almost warm,
in late November,
yet pull on my Canyon-kid-knit hat,
in browns and oranges,
to keep my wet head company,
and warm.

then up to a film,
'The Yes Men Fix the World' -
with conscience, conscientious objection,
against corporate wrongdoings, -
yes, clever satire and hi-jinx with a good vibe,
and now so tired, to bed.

in the morn,
after the pools,

I linger again
on the redwood sleeping deck,

and see the Harbin village,
the 'real' one of *Mainside*,
here below, with trees in blazing colors,
orange, reds, browns, greens & yellows,
from pool area,
over red roofs,
to all the other buildings & structures, and,

way below,
beneath yet other dwellings,

the Temple's copper-green pinnacle,
3 cones up, with spiny, spiky,
dark-golden, metal, sun orb, radiating atop,

and, just beyond, the gorgeous
elliptical arc of the
valley's entry,

a half moon,
tree-rimmed,
crescent shape,
opening upwards,

to hold the beyond-valley skies,
of light in shades of autumn-grey.

o, this watery village,
of journeying beings together,
sings to me from the pools,
in blazing, fall, falling colors.

https://scott-macleod.blogspot.com/2011/12/yellow-autumn-vineyards-blaze-below.html

Rolling Lake County Hills: I ride these hills on my way to the waters

I ride these hills on my way to the waters

I ride these hills

on my way to the waters,

the warm, daylight, dream

waters of Harbin.

Their contours create

streams, ripples and eddies,

for meditation, on the road,

on this swervy, curvy journey,

via freedom underway.

I travel straight on to Harbin.

Cold, crisp, illuminated evening,

a beautiful, light cat, alone,

outside the Harbin

health food store,

after hours -

kitty paws prancing

on cold, black asphalt -

wants attention,

as I head for the pools.

The warm pool is

just filling up

after alligator day, -

the monthly drain, clean and fill

of the warm, water pool, -

2/3rds full, now,

and the blue, foot-wide, tile band,

all around the waterline,

with beautiful, dark,

blue diamonds, and rectangles,

and light, blue triangles, interspersed,

shine forth in the soft, night light.

This Harbin is a vivid dream.

And with the crystalline

waters of Harbin, -

this pool looks Greek,

ancient, as its waters pour

noisily in from the two,

dragon ridge-side spouts,

and from the other, hot spout,

near the hot pool room's

wall's flowers.

Time travel in

less serene now-ness?

People in these moving waters

are soaking it in.

I head in to the dressing room,

after soaking long,

brush my teeth,

and wind to bed.

The light cat is still there,

by the market, -

not Arjuna, the big,

India-philosophical, Harbin cat, ...

this one is young,

and emerging from its kitty-ness, -

(after I come through the

art-flow-walkway-sculpture), ...

and this kitty-cat

wants company,

for it's cold out.

Allergic, I walk past,

want to say hi,

pet it, commune with it,

purr together,

but I don't, because

I'll sneeze,

become short of breath,

and chew my cud,

so I walk down

the back, Stonefront

Lodge road,

with the cat following me,

crossing my path,

again and again,

seeking connection and warmth, then

leaving me at the middle parking lot.

I hope it found its way to warmth

on this beginning-winter night.

Walking this Harbin hill straight down,

I head from watery warmth,

to bed, and warm sleep,

into the part of my

diurnal, rhythm dream

I know not ...

... and, later, when we awake,

we'll head in

to soak

in virtual Harbin.

https://scott-macleod.blogspot.com/2011/12/rolling-lake-county-hills-i-ride-these.html

Amboseli: How different it is to soak at Harbin, than to realize it virtually

How different it is
to soak at Harbin,
than to realize it
virtually,
or in bodymind,
by reading,
thinking,
or viewing
multimedia,
interactively.

Writing in Maine,
over a Christmas visit, -

with long walks on beaches,
and family friends,
and red brick Portland,
and the Wadsworth-Longfellow house,
which invited me
in,
to Longfellow's poetry,
'Often I think of the beautiful town
That is seated by the sea ... '
virtually, -

I hearken
to Harbin's waters,
and warmth,
and wholeness
of being there,
from afar, ...

but, while traveling,
I'm not present,
in that place,
in those
warm
waters,
in that milieu.

As I return
west coast-wise,
I draw closer,
but Harbin's
presence,
and oneness,
are in that
fluid,
geothermal
emergence
from the earth,
in that valley,
remote from the metropole, ~
and yet still far.

A virtual Harbin
is emerging, -
like Harbin's waters, -
to generate warmth,
in multimedia,
from your bathtub,
from home,
developing with the internet, ...
but emerging organically,
as process,
in writing an
actual / virtual Harbin ethnography.

Waters of wholeness, ...
an inner immersion,
in bodymind fluids,
with relaxation response, -

and at times deeply -
is happening, all the time,
yet unparalleled,
and still awaiting,
the concert
of the Harbin pool.

https://scott-macleod.blogspot.com/2011/12/amboseli-how-different-it-is-to-soak-at.html

To the Dance or the Pools? ~ Virtually! How different it is to soak at Harbin Hot Springs, than to realize it in virtual reality

Drive them back to the wine-dark taste of home,
The smell of damsons simmering in a pot,
Jam ladled thick and steaming down the sunlight.
- Seamus Heaney

To the dance, then the pools,
first at actual Harbin, over years,
dancing free, dancing be,
dancing bee, buzzing, its own honey ~
this movement-freedom grows
with warmth and energy
in concert with the music.

Connecting with dancing begins,
connecting with dancing beings,
singing inside with freedom in rhythm,
I delight in this liberation, ~
but depends on the music too ~
Blues, Grateful Dead, jamming, Rock & Roll,
make it happen for me, actually.

Heat comes, the music closes at evening's end,
and people head to the pools,
to cool down,
to complement the body-movement jam,
with serene soaking under starlight
- and the warm waters - ease.
These Harbin warm pool waters,
this elixir of encompassing body suits ~
one's whole being received by
this geo-thermally warmed liquid, ~

we like.

Virtually?

Dancing at home - wearing the Glasses -
I'm there, and so are you,
in the Harbin Conference Center,
and people be jamming,
this be-music is hop-happening,
virtually.

I start to move here at home,
Glasses revealing new openings
through which to glide,
and around my body goes,
dancing at home, dancing my home.

How Different it is to dance at home in virtual Harbin, ~
and cool - a realization.

... "Question:
whether 'tis nobler in the mind to suffer
The slings and arrows of outrageous fortune
Or to take arms against a sea of troubles,
And by opposing end them?"
(https://poets.org/poem/hamlet-act-iii-scene-i-be-or-not-be)

Or, to head to Harbin actually or virtually,
different it is,
to seek and find freedom,
by traveling from the SF bay,
the way, the Napa Valley
wine way to Harbin,
or to find one's way
there, Virtually there,
'as if' and by multimedia,
with gorgeous visuals

on a screen, currently
what a scream!

Yet beyond this traveling difference -
a big difference - this venturing out
in bodymind, locomotively, to move through,
to see, to interact with, the world,

The Soaking in warm pool
actually, in waters there,
while being in Harbin all around,
communicating silently, communing that is,
with fellow naked soakers, is wondrous.

The Soaking in one's bathtub,
virtually, from home, Glasses on,
digital screens behind the glass,
newfangled things,
while surround-seeing in Harbin ~
Brainwave headset too to come
for communication,
Tan Le's* or
Brainfingers* (only works when able to relax) or
EEG* brainwave 'dreadlocks' ~
still wondrous
yet you don't hang out actually ~
by mingling silently in warm pool ~
or visiting quietly naked

Sunning on the Sun Deck.
Immersive both, in different ways,
the warm waters help
meditation deepen ~
release inwardly deeply ~
a relaxation response in both,
and all is one in the here and now,
consciousness changes.

Yet there's more space too
in the actual Harbin's warm pool
than in this bathtub.

How best to understand consciousness,
and this consciousness,
this Harbin consciousness,
this Harbin Heart Consciousness
of HCC - Heart Consciousness Church?

Subjective-Objective accounts,
1st person-3rd person scientific narratives ~
in the warm waters, with the Glasses,
re visually observing,
and beginning to examine neural processing ~
as sentience,
awareness,
perception and
feeling
in the brain the mind, the BodyMind?

So is this, the Body-Mind problem,
moot in the warm pool,
and consciousness all one?
Yet, poetry-wise, we be studying
how brains give rise to mind,
re neural processing,
with brainwave headsets ~
thinking about it.
So then, can minds be bodies, and
is sentience brain-meat or bodyminds?
Virtually!

And how is bodymind
consciousness - importantly - virtual,
or in what ways can we make this more so - to learn?

Further, are these neurophysiological e-states

in these hypothetical virtual brains,
conscious - digitally?

And how far does sentience extend
down the phylogenetic tree?
Won't study this here now at Harbin,
yet Tononi's integrated information theory - IIT - holds promise
- 'that consciousness is identical to a certain kind of information' -
and measurable as *Phi*, the symbol for integrated information.
How could we code this in virtual brains,
yours and mine,
film-to-3D app at the street level, cell and atomic levels,
where the 'digital' corresponds 1-1
to the brain cells and neurons and processing,
and the 'virtual' - as if with multimedia,
to the mind, - somehow conscious.
Thus we might distinguish between the
Actual-Virtual, and the Physical-Digital.
And how could brainwave headset devices best turn their
information gathering inwardly
in these regards - and from the Harbin warm pool?

Phi! ~ actual, physical, that is ~
how can we simulate this?
To virtual Phi?
And further to digital Phi?

Qualia, infinite qualities,
('the internal and subjective component of sense perceptions,
arising from stimulation of the senses by phenomena' too),
perceived by many,
in myriad ways, in many bodyminds?
At actual Harbin in the warm pool,
with brain wave headsets monitoring the brain,
might one be able to study these anew?

At home with Glasses,

and brainwave headsets,
people could talk more readily,
adding a language element
to the 'subjective,'
their 1st person accounts, - and
in studying the brain technologically,
actually-virtually & physically-digitally,
where the 'as-if' virtual experience
created by multimedia and
perceived in the brain could be
digitally developed
in virtual brains ~
in a realistic virtual earth for STEM
and brain science,
and of species, and individuals,
like you and me,
soaking, soaking, soaking
in the warm pool at Harbin,
in the bath tub at home
in real virtual Harbin,
... and yet conscious:
"To the Dance or the Pools? ~ Virtually!
How different it is to soak at Harbin Hot Springs,
than to realize it in virtual reality"!

And loving bliss neurophysiology,
uniquely Harbin warm pool generated
as it bubbles up, While soaking,
how to model thee ~
and to learn from, like a musical score?

So how to measure this with headsets,
distinguishing even between,
objectively,
the relaxation response,
the relaxation response
in the Harbin warm pool,
and brain chemistry
of neural cascades of pleasure,

and then also, Subjectively, I say,
in words?

And with machine learning, further,
on the objective, 3rd person
scientific accounts' side,
could we add cameras to cells,
wee antennae, or cameras, to atoms,
articulate DNA with awareness,
(and have George Church,* Ed Boyden* and
Karl Deisseroth* already done this?),
as well as send optogenetic signals
in from the headsets,
by further examining consciousness,
via the virtual and the real thinking,
thanks to David Chalmers*
while
in the warm pool,
or In the bath tub ~
at Harbin soaking?

And subjectively, when we're blissing,
after releasing into meditation,
after eliciting the relaxation response ~
self reported, ~
use language to talk about this?
I know it consciously when I'm blissing
in the Harbin warm pool,
when bliss is simply bubbling up.
So can we measure such,
like your conscious bliss for sure,
and bring this together with what we say about this ~
with our awareness, consciousness that is,
in an account of infinite qualities, as information?

Long way to go to measure
integrated information *Phi* in the brain,
to code it in virtual brains,

to hypothesize this further,
and then objectively and 3rd person-wise
observe this scientifically (& consciously)
in the brain,
but maybe nakedness,
Actually, and
Virtually,
and examining desire,
further, too, will open ways ...

So first the dance, then the pools
this time, and,
How Different it is to Soak at Harbin, than to Realize it in Virtual Reality.

Understanding consciousness
and realizing bliss further,
connectedness,
in complement with scientific sentience,
thanks to Harbin.

To the Dance or the Pools? ~
Virtually!
How different it is to soak at
Harbin Hot Springs,
than to realize it in virtual reality.

https://scott-macleod.blogspot.com/2019/11/chameleon-vision-poem-to-dance-or-pools.html

Moon setting: Coming home under the moon

Coming Home

Coming home
under the moon
near the redwoods
in Canyon.
Feel the coolness &
its peaceful quietness.

https://scott-macleod.blogspot.com/2010/03/moon-setting-coming-home-under-moon.html

Day's California brightness and Harbin brilliance resound

Coming home
under the moon
near the redwoods
by bubbling brook
in Canyon,
feel the coolness and
its peaceful quietness.

Day's California
brightness
and Harbin brilliance
resound.

https://scott-macleod.blogspot.com/2010/03/days-california-brightness-and-harbin.html

NOTES ON THE POEMS

In these virtual actual-virtual Harbin poems, the following are places on the Harbin Hot Springs' property in northern California: Mainside, the Pool Area, and Stonefront Lodge (which burned down in 2015).

And Watsu refers to water shiatsu, a kind of water dance, and therapeutic modality, significantly developed at Harbin.

Bodymind is a word I use in these poems to join the often dualistic separation, linguistically, of the words body and mind, and also to refocus connotations of consciousness with regards to the mind-body problem, and in relation to Heart Consciousness Church, aka Harbin Hot Springs. The word *oneness* in these poems has been significant at Harbin over the years in these regards as well. See, for example, Harbin's founder Ishvara's book "Oneness In Living: Kundalini Yoga, the Spiritual Path, and the Intentional Community" as well as this pamphlet "Heart Consciousness Church - 1975-2015 - 40 Years of Living the Future - Harbin Hot Springs" - http://www.harbin.org/wp-content/uploads/2015/01/Harbin_40th_anniversary.pdf.

Ötzi, who lived who lived between 3400 and 3100 BCE, is the natural mummy ice man found in 1991 in Switzerland (https://en.wikipedia.org/wiki/Ötzi).

Here is an example of the Nyckelharpa (keyed fiddle) played by Olov Johansson in the Swedish band "Väsen Street" https://youtu.be/tWorsJwzycw (in 2009) in Minnesota, in the poem "Bug on wildflower: Into the warm water hole of Harbin, not the worm hole, New Age, Nyckelharpa."

In the last poem "To the Dance or the Pools? ~ Virtually! How different it is to soak at Harbin Hot Springs, than to realize it in virtual Reality," and with regards to science and studying consciousness -

George Church -
"DNA: George Church at TEDxCERN" 2013 - https://youtu.be/KWSYtgTLQFw ; "George Church on reversing aging | ApplySci @ Harvard" (12/10/2019) - https://youtu.be/yefzqDpJ5Oc

Ed Boyden -
"Ed Boyden: Expansion microscopy -- A new tool in brain research" (2015) - https://youtu.be/NeIhXVEITHM ; "Ed Boyden: A light switch for neurons" (2011) - https://youtu.be/hupHAPF1fHY

Karl Deisseroth -
"Karl Deisseroth (Stanford / HHMI): Development of Optogenetics" (2016) - https://youtu.be/MUGky_QaaV0

David Chalmers -
"David Chalmers on the virtual and the real" (2017) - https://youtu.be/QMLojOcOJFI ; "The Virtual and the Real" (2017 paper) - http://consc.net/papers/virtual.pdf

are innovative Harvard, MIT, Stanford, and NYU professors respectively, and here are some examples of their thinking in video , and in one paper, with regards to this poem.

In "To the Dance or the Pools? ~ Virtually! ... " I've added a blog link with every poem, where in these blog posts, you will also find photographs.

Names of poems with natural images in beginning of title are sometimes related to the poem, and sometimes arbitrary.

The cover photo's avatar is that of an UC Berkeley Asian American undergraduate student who came into the 3D virtual reality world of Second Life with me in 2009 to make this video. See, too: "Aphilo Scott MacLeod The Making of Virtual Harbin Introduction" - https://youtu.be/3nhvcHw54GE.

Thanks again to the startup Poetry Press at World University & School, which has once again kindly published my book. http://worlduniversityandschool.org/AcademicPress.html
http://scottmacleod.com/
https://twitter.com/scottmacleod ~

ABOUT THE AUTHOR

Scott MacLeod is a professor of anthropology, founder and president of the virtual wiki World University and School. He is the author of the books "Naked Harbin Ethnography: Hippies, Warm Pools, Counterculture, Clothing-Optionality and Virtual Harbin" (2016), "Haiku~ish and Other, Loving, Hippy, Harbin Poetry" (2017), "Winding Road Rainbow: Harbin, Wandering & the Poetry of Loving Bliss" (2018), and "To the Dance or the Pools? ~ Virtually! How different it is to soak at Harbin Hot Springs, than to realize it in virtual Reality."

Scott MacLeod, author (credit: Scott MacLeod)

Jacket design: Scott MacLeod
Cover photo: Scott MacLeod
Author photo: Scott MacLeod

Poetry Press at World University and School
ISBN: 978-0-578-62549-2 (Academic Press at World University and School)

www.ingramcontent.com/pod-product-compliance
Lightning Source LLC
Chambersburg PA
CBHW022119040426
42450CB00006B/759